L'E'LE' GANCE ORGANICS: THE BENEFITS OF SEA MOSS

Author
MORENNA STEWART

Published by CAE Publications www.caenterprises.online.

Table of Content

SEA MOSS

I began my Sea Moss journey in the year 2018. I was in the worst condition, concerning my health mentally, physically, and spiritually. I was diagnosed by my doctor with high blood pressure, high cholesterol, hypertension, pre-diabetic, under-active thyroid and I was 200 plus pounds overweight. My skin was irritated with dark-aging spots, open pores, and inflammation. My hair was damaged and breaking off. I was broken, but by God's grace, I am restored.

After I received my diagnosis, I began researching natural healing remedies. I discovered the healing properties of Sea Moss from Dr. Sebi, who brought international attention to this Superfood. It was a game-changer for me. I have always preferred the natural and alternative way of healing, as opposed to taking prescribed medications. I learned food can be medicine for the body when eating healthy foods with nutrients and healing properties. I changed my eating habits, which included an alkaline, low-salt, and low-calorie diet recommended by my doctor. I also included my Sea Moss gels in my daily meals. I change my lifestyle because it was detrimental to my health. I began creating additional Sea Moss products combined with herbs to help fight against my illnesses. The organic Sea Moss products I created became a part of my healing journey.

As of 2023, I am no longer taking any prescribed medications. I am my most valuable self. Sea Moss has played a pivotal role in improving my health. Sea Moss helped reduced my high cholesterol, improved my thyroid gland, and reduced the risk of any diabetes and heart diseases. Those who are privately suffering, embarrassed by your health conditions, or afraid to ask for support; I pray this information will be an encouragement to help improve your lifestyle. I would like to share with you the knowledge of Sea Moss, the wisdom of its natural healing benefits, and the understanding of how my health was repaired and my life was restored, mind, body, and spirit.

What is Sea Moss?

Sea Moss was the ocean's best-kept secret. It started gaining more popularity worldwide, in the last four years, especially during the COVID-19 pandemic. Sea Moss is a type of seaweed, also known as algae. It is found in ocean waters around the world. It grows along the coast of the Atlantic Ocean, South America, Africa, and the Caribbean. Sea Moss is also harvested in the Caribbean, along the shorelines on Sea Moss farms. It is scientifically known as Chondrus Crispus, and it contains 92 of the 102 minerals and vitamins in our bodies. Sea Moss has a high mineral content of Iodine, Calcium, Manganese, Zinc, Potassium, and protein. Potassium is one of the most important minerals for the human body. It performs by improving your gut health and boosting the immune system. It is also considered to be nature's multivitamin, containing vitamins A, K, E, C, D, B2, and B12.

Sea Moss also provides anti-viral, anti-microbial, and anti-inflammatory properties. Now imagine receiving all of these benefits with just two tablespoons of Sea Moss daily!

Sea Moss has been used for centuries in traditional medicine to treat various illnesses. It is one of the healthiest sources of nutrients in the world. It helps treat illnesses such as cancer, thyroid issues, diabetes, and mental health issues. It also helps remove excess mucus from our bodies by creating a protective film around the mucus membrane. Mucus is a phlegm-like substance, whose purpose is to protect the body from outside threats and diseases. When the mucus membrane is compromised, there is an increased production of mucus in the body. The increase in production begins to cause diseases in the body, such as lung issues, heart diseases, inflammation, and a weakened immune system.

Sea Moss is an excellent source of vitamins, minerals, and antioxidants. It grows in a variety of colors, such as purple, red, brown, gold, and green. Sea Moss is a good source of potassium chloride, omega-3 fatty acids, and chlorophyll, all of which help reduce inflammation in the respiratory and lymphatic systems. Sea Moss has the highest source of Iodine and Selenium than any other food on the planet. It helps improve your thyroid health. It helps the body to maintain mental and emotional function. The Iodine in Sea Moss strengthens the brain and central nervous system. This helps you to stay sharp with mental focus and clarity. Here are some of my favorite benefits of Sea Moss that have played an important role in my healing journey. So let's get into some of the natural benefits of Sea Moss.

High Blood Pressure

Sea Moss has been shown to improve cardiovascular health. It helps control and regulates your blood pressure. High blood pressure is the force of your blood pushing against the walls of your blood vessels. This may be caused by heart diseases, family history, being overweight, from a high salt diet, alcohol, or stress. A study done in Japan found Sea Moss showed evidence in lowering blood pressure. It is one of the main sources of Omega-3 Fatty Acids, known for lowering the risk of heart disease. It reduces blood clots, high cholesterol, and high blood pressure. Sea Moss also slows down the deterioration of blood vessels.

In 2018, I was diagnosed with high blood pressure and high cholesterol. I was hospitalized and put on four types of blood pressure medications: Lisinopril, Metoprolol, Simvastatin, and Amlodipine. I was advised by my doctor to change my entire lifestyle.

The decisions I was making were detrimental to my health. So, I began my research and discovered the numerous benefits of Sea Moss. I also changed my meal plans to a low-salt and low-calorie diet. I cut out all alcohol consumption, along with pork, high sodium, and fried foods. I added more greens and vegetables, limited myself to only fish, chicken, and beef. In addition, I added Sea Moss to my diet. My blood pressure levels return to normal, due to my faith, discipline, and eating the proper foods. In addition, I am no longer taking any prescribed blood pressure medications.

Diabetes

In my research, I further discovered Sea Moss contains phloroglucinol. The phloroglucinols found in Sea Moss have anti-diabetic properties. It helps improve your glucose metabolism. It also contains a polymer called Alginic Acid, which is known to help alleviate your blood sugar levels and enhance your insulin absorption. You are more likely to develop diabetes due to obesity and lack of exercise. Another ingredient found in Sea Moss is Fucoxanthin, which not only fights against cancer, but also helps reduce the spikes, blood sugar. Sea Moss also decreases the cholesterol levels in type 1 and type 2 diabetic patients. This is due to the Zinc content found in Sea Moss.

This information was pivotal for me because I was diagnosed with borderline diabetes.

The thyroid is responsible for regulating your hormones.

A thyroid imbalance can result in fibroid tumors and menstrual irregularities. It may also cause reproductive issues. When I was diagnosed with an underactive thyroid, I began to gain weight. The Iodine helped improve the health of my thyroid. I began creating different products to consume Sea Moss. So, I created an organic Sea Moss Energy Juice in several fruit flavors. Along with the benefits of Iodine, my Sea Moss Energy Juices also contain vitamins A, E, B2, and B12. It detoxifies and energizes you throughout your day. As a result, I no longer take the Levothyroxine prescription that treats hypothyroidism.

Weight Loss

When I learned about the weight loss benefits of Sea Moss, I discovered the carrageenan content.

This is used as a thickener and a stabilizer in both the food and beauty industry. It also acts as a fiber-soluble and promotes digestive health. Sea Moss reduces your cravings and decreases your appetite, due to the feeling of fullness. Sea Moss is vegan and low in calories. It helps pull toxins and bad bacteria from the body. The body resistance to insulin causes belly fat and prevents us from getting that desired six-pack. The Iodine in Sea Moss also produces thyroid hormones. The thyroid is responsible for the control of your metabolism. It also works as a gentle laxative that helps with constipation and eliminates waste. The Iodine in Sea Moss also helps boost your metabolism, increases your energy, and speeds up your weight loss journey.

Fluctuations in the thyroid function can lead to hormonal imbalance and slow down the metabolism.

I began to noticeably lose weight without exercising, because of the increased intake of my Sea Moss Gels and Energy drinks. Once I got my weight under control my blood levels returned to normal. I was cleared to add an exercise program and to further improve my health. I walk a minimum of 4 days a week up to two miles. My cholesterol levels were reduced, and I lost over 30 pounds.

Training & Recovery

Sea Moss is a natural bodybuilder. It helps maintain advance nerves and muscle function. It is rich in protein and helps build muscle mass. It is an excellent source of nutrients and minerals for athletes. Sea Moss also contains an amino acid called taurine, which helps burn fat and builds body muscles. The taurine found in Sea Moss speeds up the recovery process after training and exercising. It replaces the minerals and vitamins you lose during your various workouts. It decreases the inflammation and swelling in your muscles and joints. The Magnesium in Sea Moss contracts and relaxes the muscles properly. There is also collagen contained in the Sea Moss that strengthens and repairs the micro-tears in the muscles. Sea Moss helps rebuild and strengthens your body. It also accelerates the recovery of your body post-surgery.

I was diagnosed with an underactive thyroid, and I was overweight. I implemented an exercise program to help me reach my weight loss goals. The taurine in Sea Moss also helps maintain the electrolyte balance in your cells and provides proper hydration. I added my organic Sea Moss Gummy Bears also to help restore the vitamins and minerals, lost during my workouts. It replenished the nutrients I lost during my training. My organic Sea Moss Gummy Bears is a multivitamin, combined with Bladderwrack, and Burdock Root. They have a fruity flavor and are safe for kids to include in their diet.

Cancer

Sea Moss has been found to combat cancer and limit tumor growth. It contains a high content of the molecule ellagic acid. This helps prevent cancer from spreading throughout your body. The carotenoid Fucoxanthin found in Sea Moss helps fight free radicals that cause cell damage. The carotenoid is extracted from the Sea Moss by scientists, to help develop and create new prescription medicines for cancer treatment. Sea Moss was discovered along the coral reefs where anti-cancer properties have been discovered. Researchers believe that Sea Moss may provc to be essential for treating cancer patients. The mineral Selenium contains anti-carcinogenic properties. The Sea Moss contains compounds that inhibit the growth of some human cancer cell lines. The phytonutrient Algin found in Sea Moss helps prevent radiation poison. It helps pull heavy metals out of the tissues of our bodies after chemotherapy treatment.

Sea Moss helps heal the entire body by detoxing heavy metals from the tissues, the mucus membrane, the cells, and the digestive tract.

Dementia and Alzheimer

Dementia is an impairment of memory that is caused by the loss of nerve cells. When this begins to happen, the brain begins to fail. The most common cause of Dementia is Alzheimer, which is a neurodegenerative disease. It is caused by insulin resistance in the body. The Chromium found in Sea Moss lowers the resistance and enhances the performance of insulin. It is also powerful in removing corrosion, crystallization, and toxins from the brain. Sea Moss can improve brain function and memory due to the high level of the mineral Magnesium. This mineral protects the brain from damage and helps improve memory and reduces anxiety. Sea Moss also contains a high content of iodine, which strengthens the brain and the central nervous system. It helps you stay sharp, with mental focus, and clarity.

Dementia and Alzheimer affect many of our family members. This disease affected my family, my father passed away from Dementia. There is no scientific evidence that this would have saved his life. I do believe with the healing benefits of Sea Moss; it would have prolonged and improved his health. Those diagnosed with Dementia experienced hallucinations and severe loss of memory. They feel powerless and sometimes find it hard to complete their thoughts. Most Dementia patients can still be alert and aware of their condition. It is important to support and empathize with your loved ones. Along with faith, it is never too late to implement Sea Moss in their diet and to help improve their health.

Immunity Health

The immune system is one of the body's most important systems. It protects the body against infections and diseases and helps fight off any infections in the body. Sea Moss helps fight against viruses and microbial infections of the body. It also lowers inflammation and strengthens the immune response. Sea Moss is rich in Iodine, which is a necessary element in releasing antibodies in our system. These antibodies help our bodies fight against viruses, bacteria, and germs. Sea Moss helps fight against colds and flu-like symptoms such as sore throats, coughs, fever, bronchitis, and pneumonia.

Sea Moss is natures multi-vitamin. It contains numerous minerals and vitamins our bodies are composed of. It is my first go-to when it comes to immune health. I included Sea Moss in my 3-year-old grandson's daily diet.

He is 3 years old, and Sea Moss has helped limit the number of visits to the doctor. Normally, any outbreak of colds or infections in the daycare he attends, my grandson usually is not affected by it. The Iodine and vitamin C help keep his immune system protected. He has been taking Sea Moss since the age of one. He loves my fruit flavor Sea Moss gels, which he calls applesauce.

Anxiety and Depression

Depression is a mental disorder that occurs with the depletion of dopamine and serotonin. Sea Moss may help support mental health due to its high content of Potassium and vitamin B. Potassium is known to relieve symptoms of depression and tension. Vitamin B is known to support the nervous system and moderate the stress response of the body. The mineral Selenium, which is found in Sea Moss reduces the symptoms of depression. It helps regulate mood swings and provide sleep quality. The Magnesium in Sea Moss eases anxiety and helps reduce stress. The vitamin D in Sea Moss plays a crucial role in affecting your mood. It also helps with mood swings. If you find yourself feeling depressed, it may be from the deficiency of vitamin D. If there is a low level of this mineral, it could result in stressful conditions like headache, fatigue, and physical stress.

It also helps regulate brain functions by disrupting neurotransmitters.

In 2018, I was diagnosed with anxiety and depression after my divorce. My cup was full and my mind, body, and spirit collapsed under the weight of my burdens. I never really dealt with my reality during that time. My stress levels were at an all-time high. I had a son graduating from high school and a daughter who was an athlete, who both depended on me. I had to continue to push forward as a single mother. I buried the traumatic experiences from my past and continued to provide for my children and their needs. I discovered Sea Moss helps decrease depressive symptoms and reduces anxiety, so I began taking the gel. This was to help me cope with my anxiety and reduce the stress from my day-to-day routine.

Skin Health

Sea Moss is a powerhouse for your skin. Sea Moss contains minerals and vitamins E, zinc, and Magnesium. Sea Moss helps to treat psoriasis and eczema. It decreases inflammation in the skin and prevents acne. The high content of sulfur found in Sea Moss has antibacterial, antiviral, and antimicrobial properties. It also helps reduce oily skin. It reduces the increased production of sebum. Sea Moss is compelling for skin care and helps repair the skin microbiome. Sea Moss mineralizes and detoxifies your skin. It also helps your skin produce collagen and keratin. This increases your skin elasticity and prevents wrinkles. Sea Moss adds suppleness to your skin, along with a youthful glow. It also moisturizes and softens your skin. Sea Moss has vitamins C and E, which help protect the skin from UV damage. Furthermore, Sea Moss helps unclogged pores, hydrates skin, and fades dark spots.

After researching Sea Moss, I discovered it is the most potent weapon for skin care. It is combined with natural skin ingredients and organic essential oils. It is sensitive to the skin and can be applied to my skin topically. I developed an all-natural and organic Sea Moss Revitalizing Skin Moisturizer and a Sea Moss Herbal Mask.

Herbal Collection

Along with discovering the benefits of Sea Moss, I also discovered the healing properties of healing herbs and medicinal plants that naturally heal our bodies, without further damage and with minimal side effects. I began adding medicinal herbs to my Sea Moss gels, juices, and gummy bears to enhance the benefits and improved my overall health. I have always preferred natural and holistic medicine on my journey to healing. After seeing the benefits, I launched my Sea Moss Fruit Flavor Herbal Gels. I wanted to share the knowledge about the natural healing properties it contained. My Sea Moss Fruit Flavor Herbal Gels are combined with organic fruits and herbs. My purpose is to help others improve their health by sharing the knowledge I gained during my preventive care process. My organic Sea Moss Herbal Gels are combined with ayurvedic herbs combined with sweet and delicious fruits.

These fruits include Papayas, Dragon fruits, Pomegranate, Soursop, and Blueberries, along with other delicious fruits. The superfoods and ayurvedic herbs I use in my Herbal Sea Moss Gels are Ashwagandha, Maca Root, Spirulina, Moringa, Black Seed Oil, Bladderwrack, and Burdock Root, just to name a few.

Ashwagandha is a native to India where it grows wild. It is an adaptogen known as a winter cherry or Indian ginseng. The adaptogens are believed to help resist physical and mental stress. It helps calm the brain, reduces swelling, and lowers your blood pressure. Additionally, it reduces stress, and anxiety and promotes overall health and wellness. This ayurvedic herb is a superfood, due to the numerous benefits it contains.

Maca Root is a plant that grows in Peru on the high plateaus of Andres Mountain. The ayurvedic herb is also an adaptogen that helps the body manage environmental stress. It is Peruvian ginseng that contains high levels of Iron and Iodine. The dopamine contained in Maca Root helps reduce feelings of depression. It also helps stimulate the body's stress protection system. It contains all eight essential amino acids and is also considered an aphrodisiac.

Spirulina is blue-green algae with a potent source of phytonutrients, Cooper, Iron, Manganese, Iodine, and Potassium. It is rich in essential minerals, and it grows in both salt and fresh water. It is used by NASA astronauts when traveling in space. Spirulina is a superfood that includes compounds and antioxidants giving it the blue-green color.

It has a powerful plant-based protein called phycocyanin. This reduces inflammation in the body, blocks tumor growth, and kills cancer cells. It is a powerful detoxifier, which helps remove heavy metals from the body such as lead, arsenic, and mercury. These heavy metals are consumed in our foods and drinking water. It contains chlorophyll, which helps cleanse the body of toxins. It reduces the body's consumption of high cholesterol and lowers your blood pressure. It also helps reduce hypertension and boosts your energy levels. Spirulina may enhance your exercise performance. It also clears the arteries and reduces heart diseases and blood clots. Furthermore, it increases the nitric oxide in your body which helps your blood vessels relax. The vitamins E, C, and B6 boost the production of white blood, cells, and antibodies, and help fight viruses and bad bacteria in the body.

Spirulina also helps fight against the COVID-19 virus. The extract found in Spirulina may prevent patients from getting severely ill. If given to the patient at the diagnosed stage, cytokine storms can be prevented. Spirulina also contains C-phycocyanin, a protein, which enhances anti-oxidation, anti-inflammation, and anti-tumor properties. Cytokine storm occurs when the immune cells are hyperactive, and it causes the body to attack itself. It is responsible for the critical cases of COVID-19. Spirulina reduces 70 percent of the immune system protein TNF-a, which causes a dangerous cytokine storm in the lungs. This can lead to acute respiratory distress syndrome and irreversible organ damage.

Moringa is rich in phytonutrients, minerals, vitamins, and antioxidants. It is a plant native to India and has proteins to help fight inflammation and reduce pain. It is also called the Tree of

Life because it has been discovered to unscientifically cure over 300 illnesses and diseases. It is used for food and medicines. It is high in protein and contains 8 out of 9 essential Amino Acids. It helps fight malnutrition due to its drought resistance. It can grow anywhere in the world and any climate conditions. It is one of the most nutritional plants in the world. It includes 27 vitamins and 46 antioxidants. The antioxidants help reduce oxidative stress. It has been used in ayurvedic healing for centuries. It contains Calcium, Potassium, Magnesium, and vitamin C. It is anti-inflammatory and anti-bacterial. It reduces high blood pressure, lowers cholesterol, and helps with digestion. Moringa also contains flavonoids and polyphenols, which fight against premature wrinkles. These compounds have a high content of anti-aging benefits for skincare.

Black Seed Oil is made from the seed of the nigella sativa plant, also known as the black cumin plant. It is native to southwestern Asia, Africa, and the Mediterranean. It can be used as herbal medicine or spice. Black seed oil is one of the most potent sources of antioxidants, which helps people lose weight. It helps the body burn its fat reserves for energy. Black seed oil helps support those with diabetes with beta cells located in the pancreas. This also helps produce insulin. It can help reduce the size of cancerous tumors and prevent the spreading of cancerous cells. Additionally, it is antiviral, antibacterial, and antifungal. It helps to fight off cold and flu-like symptoms. It has also been discovered that Black Seed Oil helps improve the natural function of the liver. It helps by detoxifying harmful chemicals from the body.

Bladderwrack is used to make natural medicine. It is native to the Atlantic and Pacific oceans and the North Sea and Baltic Sea. The vitamins and minerals reduce the risk of heart attack and stroke by strengthening the blood vessels. It has one the richest content of Iodine and helps the body to lose weight. It contains vitamin A, which is rich in beta-carotene.

It reduces swelling in the body due to its anti-inflammatory properties. Bladderwrack reduces the risk of cancerous cells with the fucoidan ingredient it contains. The Alginic acid it contains helps relieve constipation and improves gut health.

Burdock Root is a vegetable native to Europe and northern Asia. It has been used for centuries in holistic medicine. It has Vitamin B, Magnesium, Calcium, vitamin C, Iron, and Zinc. It detoxes impurities in the bloodstream and eliminates toxins through the skin.

It is a blood purifier and helps prevent certain cancers. Burdock Root also contains powerful antioxidants, including quercetin, luteolin, and phenolic acids. The antioxidants protect the cells in the body from damage due to free radicals. It also protects the liver and lymphatic system from damage. It helps reduce high blood sugar. Additionally, the Burdock Root contains fiber and polyphenols, which helps control blood sugar levels. It is also often used as a diuretic and digestive aid. Additionally, Burdock Root helps grow and strengthen your hair. It contains Arctiine, which restores the normal hair growth cycle and promotes hair growth. The vitamin A in Burdock Root nourishes the scalp and strengthens the hair follicles. It also helps strengthen the natural hair shaft.

Valerian Root is native to Europe, parts of Asia, and North America.

It is a woody plant that has been shown to increase the levels of gamma-aminobutyric acid. It helps regulate nerve cells, providing a calming effect on the nervous system. It helps battle insomnia and eases anxiety and psychological stress. This is due to its content of valerenol and valeric acid found in the root. It increases mental alertness and cognitive function in elderly patients with dementia. Valerian has powerful antispasmodic properties, which help reduce excitability, a hysterical state, and the fear of illness, by acting as a sedative. It helps lowers blood pressure and reduces hypertension caused by stress. Additionally, it is a powerful aphrodisiac.

Restoration Plan

What is detoxification?

Detoxification is a natural cleansing of the body. It is the removal of toxins and pollutants from within the cells. Detoxification removes impurities from the bloodstream of the liver, kidney, lungs, skin cells, and some mucus membranes. It is fasting from your normal daily diet. Toxins are found in our foods, the water we drink, and the hair and skin products we use. A detox is removing toxins at a high level, such as those stored in cells. It is regulated by the liver system and by the endocrine systems.

When should you detox?

It is a good time to detox, when the endocrine system, immune system, and nervous system are not properly working. Improper diets cause diseases, such as high blood pressure, high cholesterol, diabetes, and cell damage.

The body begins to experience unexplained fatigue, and you feel unmotivated, depressed, and lacking energy. If you are struggling with skin irritation, digestion, sleep disorders, and cravings notifies the body it is time to detox. These systems all help to remove toxins from the body and make the liver and kidney function more efficiently. It flushes out impurities and helps with weight loss. The process helps to restore skin health and provides anti-aging benefits. It gets rid of blemishes, acne, and skin irritations. It boosts your energy levels and helps improve mental health and fitness.

How to detox spiritually?

Detox is not only just for the body, but it is beneficial to the spirit. Praying and meditating are one of the most powerful methods of cleansing the soul. Many things happen in our daily lives that poison our spirits. There are losses we experience in our daily lives. We experienced the loss of loved ones, loss of income, and loss of a home or a divorce. We sometimes need a reset and restore to obtain a peaceful state of our mind. These losses can drain us mentally and spiritually. One of the most important methods for me is meditating on the word of God. I would also listen to worship music during my daily walks. For me, this helps maintain calmness and peace in my life. It helps renew my mindset and bring about clarity and focus.

What exercises should I do during detoxification?

You may choose whatever exercises that may work best for you. There are numerous health benefits to adding physical activities to your daily routine. I recommend you speak with your physician and decide what would be best for you. There are several options to begin an exercise routine. You can join a gym and speak with a personal trainer. You can begin walking, riding a bike, yoga exercises, or running. It all depends on what makes you comfortable. Exercising can help lose weight, fight against health diseases, and helps boost your energy.

How long should you detox?

There are numerous detox programs on the market. Typically, the standard detox is 7 to 10 days. There are 3 days: 7 days, 10 days, 14 days, and 21 days detox programs. It all depends on your preference and your personal goals. The decision should be based on your health and what personal goals you would like to attain. I recommend you speak with your physician, depending on your health. I did a 15-day detox plan.

What to eat during a detox?

There are several ways to detox your body. The only true detox fasting is with water for a certain time. In the first two weeks, I consumed my Sea Moss Herbal Detox Cleanser first thing in the morning. Throughout my day, I also consume 6 to 12 bottles a day of the Sea Moss Energy Juices and gels, I created. Each bottle contains 12 ounces. In week three, I only consume my Sea Moss Fruit Flavor Gels and fresh fruits. The 15-day detox plan helped cleanse my body, helped me loosed weight, and helped to remove toxins from my body. It contains proteins, vitamins, and minerals. It also provides a source of nutrients. Furthermore, it contains anti-inflammatory and antioxidant properties.

My Sea Moss Energy Detox Juices:

My Sea Moss Herbal Detox Cleanser:

-5 Fruit Flavors
-Cascara Sagrada
-Agave Syrup
-Mullein
-Cayenne Pepper
-Rhubarb Root
-My Sea Moss Alkaline Water
-Other Organic Ingredients

The Sea Moss Herbal Detox Cleanser should be lukewarm and consumed within 15 minutes of drinking. I consumed no solid foods during the fast. Depending on your medical conditions you can add fresh fruits or a raw vegan diet. There was no alcohol consumption, smoking, sugar, no solid foods, or dairy products. The fast should be done for at least a minimum of 7 days to no more than 40 days.

After completing your detox, you should start with orange juice, fresh fruits, vegetables, and light soups with no meat for the first several days. I would also suggest doing a detox at least every 3 months.

After completing my 10-day detox fast, I lost over 30 pounds. I continue to follow my low-calorie and low-salt diet provided by my doctor. Sea Moss will always be a daily source of nutrients for me. My skin is glowing, and my hair is healthy. My mindset has been renewed and full of clarity and my body is free of prescription medicines. I gained so much knowledge on my healing journey. I plan to implement the new eating habits I pick up along the way. I also provided a list of food groups as a guideline for healthier eating.

List of Foods:

Vegetables:
Cabbage
Garlic
Avocados
Kale
Collard Greens
Bell Peppers
Cucumbers
Onions
Spinach
Tomatoes
Turnips
Asparagus
Sweet Potatoes
Okra

Oils:
Peanuts, Cashews, Walnuts, Sesame Seeds, Avocado Oil, Brazilian Nuts, Hempseed Oil, Vegan Cheese

Fish:
Salmon, Tuna, Grouper, Tofu

Grains:
Quinoa, Brown Rice, Black Rice, Granola

Teas:
Ginger, Raspberry, Lemon, Moringa, Sea Moss, Chamomile, Anise

Fruits:
Strawberries
Blueberries
Grapes
Cherries
Raspberries
Papaya
Lemons
Limes
Plums
Peaches
Coconuts
Soursop
Dragon fruit
Watermelon
Pears
Melons
Dates
Mango
Pineapples
Apples

Seasoning and Spices:
Sea Salt
Cracked Black Pepper
Garlic
Onion
Cumin
Sage
Kelp
Bay Leaves
Vegan Seasoning
Thyme
Turmeric
Oregano
Cayenne Pepper

Meats:
Chicken, Vegan Steak, Shrimp, Beef, Eggs, Chicken Andouille Sausage

Sweet Flavors:
Pure Agave Syrup, Dates, Brown Suga, Raw Honey

This is a list of foods I include in my everyday meal plans and what works for me.

I recommend you research what kind of foods you like and find a healthier choice based on you and your family likes. For example, I love a nice piece of steak, so I research and learned about vegan steak. After trying out a few brands, I found the one that works for me. This was added to my list as a healthier version. In addition, I eliminated a lot of processed foods and sugars from my current diet. Instead of sugar, I use agave syrup or raw honey as a sweetener.

Conclusion

Sea Moss is a powerful superfood with numerous benefits to help improve your health. It removes toxins from the body, decreases bad bacteria in the gut, and reduces the risk of chronic diseases. In 2018, I was sick mentally, physically, and spiritually. I researched alternative ways to heal my body, aside from taking chemicals that can cause further damages. I pray the knowledge and information provided in this book will get you started on your journey of healing. When writing this book it gave me opportunity to share my personal experience on how my health was restored through faith, changing my eating habits, and renewing my mindset. Along my journey of healing, I started a Sea Moss business. I launched L'Elegance Skin Care in 2019. I created a Sea Moss skin care moisturizer to improve the conditions of my skin. I learned the natural healing ingredients for my skin care and could also be used to repair other health issues. I created some amazing all natural Sea Moss products that may be beneficial to you and your family unit. The scariest part for me during my experience was stepping out on faith and trusting the process.

I discovered there are numerous benefits of healing properties in plants and herbs. There are medicinal properties in various trees, roots, leaves, barks and flowers around the world. These plants and herbs are found to repair skin issues, cure chronic diseases, and helps reduce stress and anxiety. Many cultures around the world still practice these medicinal traditions. Our bodies are different and may respond differently to the herbs and nutrients I used in my products. Speak to your doctor, ask questions, and begin to learn about your body. Research the illnesses and diseases you have been diagnosed with, learn about the different medicinal herbs and foods that naturally heal these conditions. I am not a doctor, and I do not recommend anyone to stopping taking any medications, because some conditions are more severe than others.

Furthermore, I learned Sea Moss has a bad reputation for its taste and texture. I wanted to remove the ocean bland taste from my gels. I created a recipe using real fruits, Wildcrafted Sea Moss and other organic ingredients. I wanted to create fun and delicious flavors, where my customers not only enjoy the taste, but enjoy the benefits also. There are many individuals who would love to add sea moss to their diet but would not enjoy the taste. I created the natural fruit flavors that allow you to enjoy my products as well as the flavors. You will experience some amazing flavors with my products, without compromising the Sea Moss and you will still receive the numerous benefits.

Disclaimer:

These statements have not been evaluated by the Food and Drug Administration. The nutritional benefits vary for each individual. The information provided should not be used for diagnosing or treating health issues or diseases. My products are not intended to cure or treat any diseases or medical issues. This information is provided for educational purposes and to share my healing journey with all of you. Please consult a licensed healthcare provider before using any of my products. These statements have not been approved by the FDA. Sea Moss should be avoided by those with an allergic reaction to Iodine. If you are pregnant or have any pre-existing conditions, please consult your healthcare provider before using Sea Moss. The information contained in this book is correct to the best of my knowledge, based on research and my personal life experiences. The author and the publisher do not assume and hereby disclaim any liability to any party for any loss, damage, or disruption caused by errors whether such errors may result from negligence, accidents or any other causes.

There are many benefits of taking sea moss daily. There are also side effects to taking Sea Moss. When consuming Sea Moss in a moderate amount it is safe to take. The recommended dose of Sea Moss is two tablespoon daily. The side effects of Sea Moss are rare, but there are still possibilities. One major concern when consuming large amounts of Sea Moss is the high content of Iodine. An overconsumption of Sea Moss increases the amount of Iodine and may result in thyroid dysfunction. Those who are allergic to Iodine should avoid taking Sea Moss. Sea Moss also has a mild laxative effect due to the Magnesium and fiber it contains. The Magnesium contained in Sea Moss may also cause weight loss.

You may also feel nausea, but there is not enough reliable information regarding these rare side effects of Sea Moss. Even though Sea Moss is a powerhouse for skin conditions, it may cause irritation, itching, or redness. Depending on where the Sea Moss was purchased, it may have been prepared incorrectly. I do not use Sea Moss powder in any of my gels, juices, water or gummies.

Sources:

-Pandolfi, Laura. "Why Is Sea Moss So Good For Blood Pressure and Heart Health." Organics Nature, 2 Nov. 2022. www.organicnature.com/blogs/news/sea-moss-for-blood-pressure-and-heart-health/.

Czerwony, R.D., Beth. "What are the benefits of Sea Moss? - Cleveland Clinic" Health Essentials, 2 Dec. 2022. https://health.clevelandclinic.org/sea-moss-benefits/.

-Burdeos, R.D., Johna. "Advertiser Disclosure The Health Benefits of Sea Moss, According To Experts." Forbes, 13 Oct. 2022. www.forbes.com/health/body/sea-moss-benefits/

-Youdim, M.D., F.A.C.P., Adrienne. "Advertiser Disclosure The Health Benefits of Sea Moss, According To Experts." Forbes, 13 Oct. 2022. www.forbes.com/health/body/sea-moss-benefits/

-Food Data Central. "Seaweed, Irish Moss, Raw." USDA, 19 Apr. 2019. https://fdc.nal.usda.gov/fdc-app.html#/food-details/168456/nutrients/

-Schneider, Jamie. "Sea Moss Can Benefit Any Skin Type: Here's How to Use It in Routine." MBG, 31, Aug. 2022. https://www.mindbodygreen.com/articles/sea-moss-benefits-for-skin/

-Laurence, Emily. "7 Benefits Of Maca Root, According to Experts." Forbes Health, 10 Jan. 2023. www.forbes.com/health/body/maca-root-benefit/.

Quintero, RD, Edibel. "Is Sea Moss Good for Diabetes: Benefits and Uses?" Health Reporter, 19 Aug. 2022. www.healthreporter.com/is-sea-moss-good-for-diabetes/.

-Vida. "Memory Boosting Herbs." Vida, 2018. https://www.Vida.com/content/memory-boostin-herbs/.

-Guideline. "The Use Of Herbal Medicines In Primary Health Care." World Health Organization, 10 Mar. 200. https://www.who.int/publication/i/item/9789241594448/.

-Herbal Vineyards. "Sea Moss: The Powerhouse of Energy." Herbal Vineyards, 26 Jul. 2021. www.herbalvineyards.com/blogs/healing101/sea-moss-the-powerhouse-of-energy/.

-Klien, Abigail. "Blue Green Spirulina Algae May Prevent Serious COVID-19." ISRAEL21c, 3 Mar. 2021. www.israel2lc.org/blue-green-spirulina algae-may-prevent-serious-covid-19.com/

-WebMD Editorial Contributors, "Spirulina: Are There Health Benefits?" NOURISH, 21, Sep. 2021. https://www.webmd.com/diet/spirulina-health-benefits/

-Chu, Will. "Algae Extract May Act to Slow down COVID Progression, say researchers." Nutra Ingredients Europe, 02 Mar. 2021. https://www.nutraingredients/Article/2021/03/02/Algae-extract-may-act-to-slow-down-COVID-progression.com/

-BioSea Health. "Cancer Fighting Properties Of Seaweed." BioSea Health, 9 Feb. 2022. https://bioseahealth.com/cancer-fighting-properties-of-seaweed/.

-BioSea Health. "Seaweed Reduces Alzheimer's?" BioSea Health, 14 Sep. 2019. *https://bioseahealth.com/cancer-fighting-properties-of-seaweed/.*

-Andrews, Karena. "Dr. Sebi Method For Cleansing and Revitalizing The Body – Steps To." Alkaline Meal Ideas And More - YouTube, 2020. *www.youtube.com/channel/UCN*

Panchal, Bhupesh. "Sea Moss Health Benefits." Holland and Barrett, 10 Jun. 2022. *www.hollandandbarrett.com/the-health-hub/food-drink/nutrition/sea-moss-health-benefits/.*

James, Kylie. "What the Difference Between a Cleanse and a Detox." YouTube, 2018 *www.korunutrition.com/what-the-difference-between-a -cleanse-and-a-detox/*

Contact the Author at:

leleganceorganicsbeautybrand@gmail.com

for products, questions, services, and speaking engagements.

www.ingramcontent.com/pod-product-compliance
Lightning Source LLC
La Vergne TN
LVHW090139160826
845673LV00017B/2520
* 9 7 8 0 9 8 8 6 1 2 9 1 4 *